Improve your practice!

Paul Harris

www.fabermusic.com/improve

© 2004 by Faber Music Ltd
First published in 2004 by Faber Music Ltd
3 Queen Square London WC1N 3AU
Design by Susan Clarke
Printed in England by Caligraving Ltd
All rights reserved

ISBN 0-571-52273-4

FABER *ff* MUSIC

Introduction

You've probably heard the expression 'practice makes perfect'. But it's not just the quantity of practice that's important; it's the quality. With the aid of *Improve your practice!*, you will begin to develop ways of making the most out of your practice sessions – however long they are. What's more, you'll also find that your wider musical skills of aural, theory, sight-reading, improvisation and composition develop alongside. And the fun playing cards are guaranteed to liven things up no end! So good luck, and let's get started ...

Here's what you do:

Before you start
Get out your scissors and cut each playing card to size. As you work through each grade, add the new cards to your deck so you have even more to choose from.

1 Be a musical detective
When you begin a new piece, first complete *Explore your piece*. You may want to fill in all the boxes in one go or spread your detective work over a week or two.

2 Warm up
Begin each practice session with some warm-ups. Your teacher will write some down on the warm-ups page for you to choose from.

3 Without music
Choose the piece you are going to focus on in your practice and deal yourself two to three cards from the 'Without music' pack. Work through the activities without looking at the music.

4 With music
Now (using the same piece) deal yourself between two to four cards from the 'With music' pack and work through those activities with the music open.

5 You choose
Complete your practice with a further activity of your own choice – playing one of your other pieces, some other scales, doing some sight-reading, composing a piece – and always be thinking about what the week's special feature might be (see page 20).

important

You may want to concentrate on just one piece in a practice session, or perhaps work at several. Deal yourself different cards for each piece.

Warm-ups

Ask your teacher to make a list of warm-ups for you to choose from when you begin each practice session (or see www.fabermusic.com/improve for some suggestions). These will include ideas on posture and hand position, playing without tension and a range of technical exercises.

Choose two or three warm-ups at the beginning of *every* practice session and spend at least two to three minutes on them.

Explore your piece

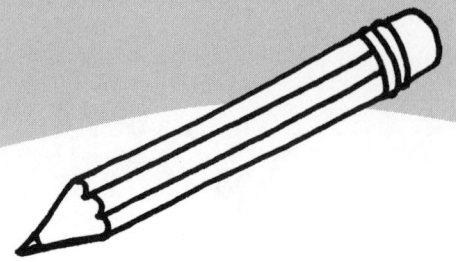

1 Title

2 Composer

3 Period

See page 24 for help

4 What does the title tell you about the music?

5 What key is the piece in? Does it change? What is the relative key?

6 Are there any scale or arpeggio patterns in the music? Which scales or arpeggios are they? In which bars do they occur?

7 Explain the time signature. Does it change?

8 What will you count?

9 Write down all the dynamics that occur (including *cresc.* and *dim.*). List them in order of soft – loud:

4

All these answers form the 'ingredients' of your piece. If you don't understand a question, don't worry: just remember to ask your teacher in your next lesson.

10 Write down any other markings (such as staccato, slurs, accents etc.) and their meanings:

11 How would you describe the character or mood of the piece? Does it change?

12 How will you communicate this in your performance?

13 Find out something interesting about the composer:

14 Find out the names of some other pieces by the composer:

15 Are there any particular rhythms or repeated rhythmic patterns in the piece? Write them down here, and then clap them:

16 Have you found anything tricky or challenging in the piece? Which bars will require special practice?

Explore your piece

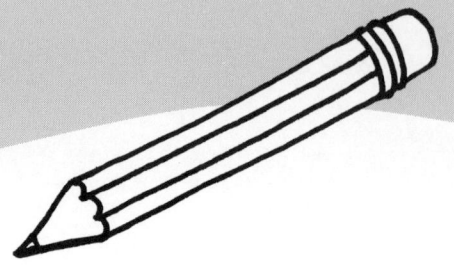

1 Title

2 Composer

3 Period

See page 24 for help

4 What does the title tell you about the music?

5 What key is the piece in? Does it change? What is the relative key?

6 Are there any scale or arpeggio patterns in the music? Which scales or arpeggios are they? In which bars do they occur?

7 Explain the time signature. Does it change?

8 What will you count?

9 Write down all the dynamics that occur (including *cresc.* and *dim.*). List them in order of soft – loud:

10 Write down any other markings (such as staccato, slurs, accents etc.) and their meanings:

11 How would you describe the character or mood of the piece? Does it change?

12 How will you communicate this in your performance?

13 Find out something interesting about the composer:

14 Find out the names of some other pieces by the composer:

15 Are there any particular rhythms or repeated rhythmic patterns in the piece? Write them down here, and then clap them:

16 Have you found anything tricky or challenging in the piece? Which bars will require special practice?

Explore your piece

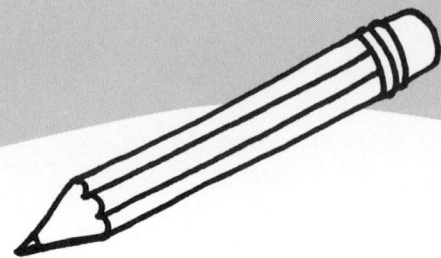

1 **Title**

2 **Composer**

3 **Period**

See page 24 for help

4 **What does the title tell you about the music?**

5 **What key is the piece in? Does it change? What is the relative key?**

6 **Are there any scale or arpeggio patterns in the music?**
   Which scales or arpeggios are they? In which bars do they occur?

7 **Explain the time signature. Does it change?**

8 **What will you count?**

9 **Write down all the dynamics that occur**
   (including *cresc.* and *dim.*). List them in order of soft – loud:

10 Write down any other markings (such as staccato, slurs, accents etc.) and their meanings:

11 How would you describe the character or mood of the piece? Does it change?

12 How will you communicate this in your performance?

13 Find out something interesting about the composer:

14 Find out the names of some other pieces by the composer:

15 Are there any particular rhythms or repeated rhythmic patterns in the piece? Write them down here, and then clap them:

16 Have you found anything tricky or challenging in the piece? Which bars will require special practice?

Explore your piece

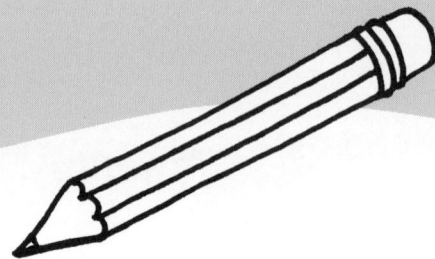

1 Title

2 Composer

3 Period

See page 24 for help

4 What does the title tell you about the music?

5 What key is the piece in? Does it change? What is the relative key?

6 Are there any scale or arpeggio patterns in the music? Which scales or arpeggios are they? In which bars do they occur?

7 Explain the time signature. Does it change?

8 What will you count?

9 Write down all the dynamics that occur (including *cresc.* and *dim.*). List them in order of soft – loud:

Explore your piece

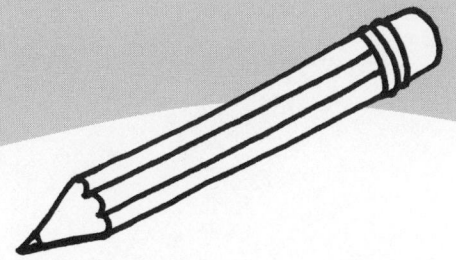

1 Title

2 Composer

3 Period

See page 24 for help

4 What does the title tell you about the music?

5 What key is the piece in? Does it change? What is the relative key?

6 Are there any scale or arpeggio patterns in the music?
Which scales or arpeggios are they? In which bars do they occur?

7 Explain the time signature. Does it change?

8 What will you count?

9 Write down all the dynamics that occur
(including *cresc.* and *dim.*). List them in order of soft – loud:

10 Write down any other markings (such as staccato, slurs, accents etc.) and their meanings:

11 How would you describe the character or mood of the piece? Does it change?

12 How will you communicate this in your performance?

13 Find out something interesting about the composer:

14 Find out the names of some other pieces by the composer:

15 Are there any particular rhythms or repeated rhythmic patterns in the piece? Write them down here, and then clap them:

16 Have you found anything tricky or challenging in the piece? Which bars will require special practice?

What key is the piece in? Improvise a short piece in this key.

Now say the names of the notes of the scale and arpeggio up and down three times, then play them. What is the relative key? What is the key beginning on the dominant note? Now play those scales and arpeggios!

Choose a dynamic level or articulation marking from section 9 or 10 of *Explore your piece*, and make up a short piece concentrating on it. Think of a title before you begin.

Try to remember the piece (perhaps writing it down so that you can practise it again).

Think about the title. What does it tell you about the character of the piece?

Now make up your own short and simple piece with the same character. Think carefully about that character, then compose another piece with the opposite character.

What is the time signature of the piece?

Make up a simple rhythm (four to eight bars in length) in this time signature. Write your rhythm down.

Now improvise a tune to fit the rhythm.

Play as much of the piece as you can from memory, including the dynamics, phrasing, and other markings. Play with character and expression. Don't worry if you can only remember a bar or two!

Choose a scale you are currently learning and play it beginning and ending with the top note.

Now practise it descending *p* and ascending *f*.

Find another piece (perhaps from your sight-reading book) that is in the same key or uses some of the same patterns as your piece. Study it silently, hearing it in your head. Practise any tricky bits and finally, feeling a strong, steady pulse, play it slowly and as accurately as possible.

Practise the scale and arpeggio of the piece slowly, with even rhythm and tone. Then combine playing the scale and arpeggio with one ingredient from *Explore your piece*.

Now make up a short piece in $\frac{4}{4}$ using the scale and arpeggio patterns you've been working on.

What colour (or colours) does the piece make you think of? Improvise a short piece that conjures up that colour!

Choose one of the rhythms from section 15 of *Explore your piece* and practise the scale of the piece using that rhythm.

Play the keynote of the piece.

Working out the notes in your head first, sing the 3rd, then the 5th note of the scale. Afterwards, play them to check how close you were!

Practise playing the first and final notes of the piece with the best tone quality you can.

WITH MUSIC

Choose a bar from section 16 of *Explore your piece*. Think about the problem carefully and then compose two or three short exercises to help you practise it: for example, by repeating a particular pattern, playing it at different speeds, or changing the rhythm. Write the exercises down if you like.

WITH MUSIC

Play the piece (or part of it) through with no expression at all.

Now play the same music with as much expression as you can, thinking about how to shape the phrases.

WITH MUSIC

Choose a short passage and then play it:

• *ff*
• *pp*
• with a *crescendo* and *diminuendo*
• much slower than marked
• at the correct tempo
• from memory

WITH MUSIC

Practise the first eight bars, beginning from bar two. Then do the same, this time beginning from bar three.

WITH MUSIC

Reading the music, hear the piece through in your head. Remember to hear the dynamics and other markings too. Make sure you know the meanings of all the markings in the piece. Now try to hear the piece in your head again – this time from memory! Imagine yourself playing it with lots of expression.

WITH MUSIC

Choose a short passage (one or two bars). Play it, listening very carefully to the melodic shape.

Now play it starting one tone lower. Now sing the same passage at any comfortable pitch.

WITH MUSIC

Can you spot any repeated patterns in the piece? They may be rhythmic or melodic; exact or slightly altered each time.

Choose one pattern and use it to compose a short piece of your own.

WITH MUSIC

Tap the rhythm of the piece with one hand and the pulse with the other. Now swap hands. Now tap the rhythm and count the beats aloud.

WITH MUSIC

Choose a few bars and play them backwards (i.e. from right to left).

WITH MUSIC

Choose as much, or as little, of the piece as you like (it may be the whole piece!). Prepare and then perform it, making sure you really communicate the character. Decide if anything could be improved and then perform it again. Think about how you might introduce the piece to an audience.

WITH MUSIC

Work at a phrase and then try to play it with your eyes closed. Listen very carefully to your playing. Is the music in four-bar or other length phrases?

WITH MUSIC

Practise a passage thinking about the character of the music. Are you successfully achieving that character? What would you like to make someone listening to your performance think or feel?

10 Write down any other markings (such as staccato, slurs, accents etc.) and their meanings:

11 How would you describe the character or mood of the piece? Does it change?

12 How will you communicate this in your performance?

13 Find out something interesting about the composer:

14 Find out the names of some other pieces by the composer:

15 Are there any particular rhythms or repeated rhythmic patterns in the piece? Write them down here, and then clap them:

16 Have you found anything tricky or challenging in the piece? Which bars will require special practice?

Explore your piece

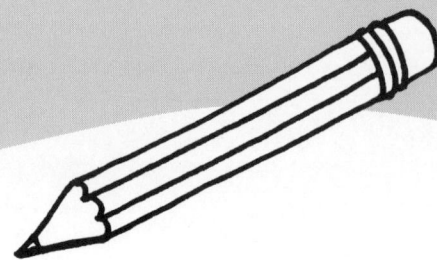

1. **Title**

2. **Composer**

3. **Period**

See page 24 for help

4. **What does the title tell you about the music?**

5. **What key is the piece in? Does it change? What is the relative key?**

6. **Are there any scale or arpeggio patterns in the music?**
   Which scales or arpeggios are they? In which bars do they occur?

7. **Explain the time signature. Does it change?**

8. **What will you count?**

9. **Write down all the dynamics that occur**
   (including *cresc.* and *dim.*). List them in order of soft – loud:

14

10 Write down any other markings (such as staccato, slurs, accents etc.) and their meanings:

11 How would you describe the character or mood of the piece? Does it change?

12 How will you communicate this in your performance?

13 Find out something interesting about the composer:

14 Find out the names of some other pieces by the composer:

15 Are there any particular rhythms or repeated rhythmic patterns in the piece? Write them down here, and then clap them:

16 Have you found anything tricky or challenging in the piece? Which bars will require special practice?

Explore your piece

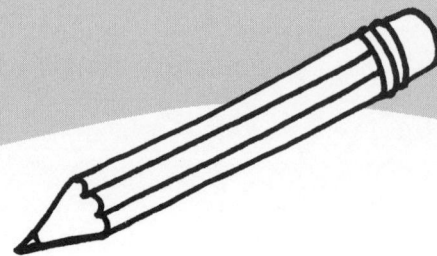

1 Title

2 Composer

3 Period

See page 24 for help

4 What does the title tell you about the music?

5 What key is the piece in? Does it change? What is the relative key?

6 Are there any scale or arpeggio patterns in the music?
Which scales or arpeggios are they? In which bars do they occur?

7 Explain the time signature. Does it change?

8 What will you count?

9 Write down all the dynamics that occur
(including *cresc.* and *dim.*). List them in order of soft – loud:

10 Write down any other markings (such as staccato, slurs, accents etc.) and their meanings:

11 How would you describe the character or mood of the piece? Does it change?

12 How will you communicate this in your performance?

13 Find out something interesting about the composer:

14 Find out the names of some other pieces by the composer:

15 Are there any particular rhythms or repeated rhythmic patterns in the piece? Write them down here, and then clap them:

16 Have you found anything tricky or challenging in the piece? Which bars will require special practice?

Explore your piece

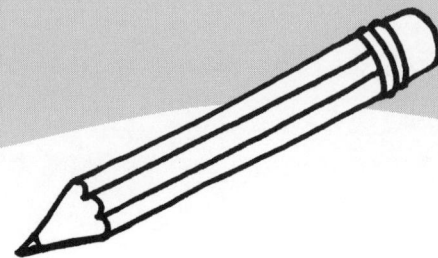

1 **Title**

2 **Composer**

3 **Period**

See page 24 for help

4 **What does the title tell you about the music?**

5 **What key is the piece in? Does it change? What is the relative key?**

6 **Are there any scale or arpeggio patterns in the music?**
Which scales or arpeggios are they? In which bars do they occur?

7 **Explain the time signature. Does it change?**

8 **What will you count?**

9 **Write down all the dynamics that occur**
(including *cresc.* and *dim.*). List them in order of soft – loud:

10 Write down any other markings (such as staccato, slurs, accents etc.) and their meanings:

11 How would you describe the character or mood of the piece? Does it change?

12 How will you communicate this in your performance?

13 Find out something interesting about the composer:

14 Find out the names of some other pieces by the composer:

15 Are there any particular rhythms or repeated rhythmic patterns in the piece? Write them down here, and then clap them:

16 Have you found anything tricky or challenging in the piece? Which bars will require special practice?

Practice diary

As your practice develops each week, decide on one special feature.
It may, for example, be one of the following:

· part or all of one of your pieces that you can play really well

· a technical challenge that you've overcome

· an improvisation (one that you can remember!)

· a particular scale you can play really well

· your own composition

Write it down in the table below and show it to your teacher.
It will become a very good starting point for the next lesson.

Week beginning	This week's special feature

Exam checklist

You may want to work through this section with your teacher.

Scales, arpeggios and broken chords List all the scales etc. you need to know for the exam, or those that you are currently working on:	*Aural* List the different tests you'll need to do:

Countdown to an exam

Tick each statement as soon as you feel it to be true! Award yourself a treat when all are ticked.

3 weeks to go …

◯ I can play all my scales slowly but accurately, rhythmically and with a good and even tone.

◯ I'm practising sight-reading every day.

◯ I know exactly what the aural tests require me to do and have had a lot of help with them.

◯ I can play my pieces fairly fluently and with expression.

2 weeks to go …

◯ I can play all my scales slowly but accurately and fluently.

◯ I'm practising sight-reading every day.

◯ I've had a lot of practice at the aural tests.

◯ I can play my pieces fluently, with expression and character.

1 week to go …

◯ I can play all my scales accurately, fluently and confidently.

◯ I'm still practising sight-reading every day.

◯ I'm confident about the aural tests.

◯ I've performed all my pieces to friends/relatives confidently and with lots of musical expression and character.

1 day to go …

◯ I'm really looking forward to the exam and am going to get a good night's sleep!

21

Useful stuff

Bear in mind that these dates are intended as a guide only.

Composer dates	Period
c.1425–1600	Renaissance
c.1600–1750	Baroque
c.1750–1820	CLASSICAL
c.1820–1915	Romantic
c.1915–2000	20th Century
2000 +	21st Century

Notes

Too tired to practise?

Then do one of the following activities instead:

1. Practise without your instrument – just sit down with the piece you're learning and hear it through in your head. Think particularly about the character of the music.

2. Listen to some music – another piece by the same composer, a piece by another composer living at the same time, or some music in the same style. Your teacher or parents will help.

3. Do a **PEP** analysis on the piece you are learning:
    P is for *problems* – decide what problems you still have to solve, technical or rhythmic for example. Make a note of them.
    E is for *expression* – what will you be trying to convey in your performance?
    P is for *practice* – the next practice! What in particular will you practise in your next session? Write your intentions down.

4. Just get your instrument out and clean it!